HEAD*lines*

by

Bernard Briggs

i

Published by

Cauliay Publishing & Distribution

PO Box 12076 Aberdeen

AB16 9AL

First Edition

ISBN 978-0-9575567-0-6

Copyright © Bernard Briggs. 2013

Cover photography and design © Mandy Briggs

A CIP catalogue record for this book is available from the British Library.

Forward

Is insanity an unhealthy vividness of thought?

- Charles Darwin

'Headlines' is my third collection of poetry, within which I have also included a few short stories. These stories have been written over a number of years and been re-written many times, before reaching the form in which you find them here. I include them because they threatened to haunt me for years to come, unless I did.

It's always interesting to me how a collection comes together to form a publishable body of work. For example the majority of poems in this volume were originally written during a (failed) attempt to write a poem a day for a whole year, based on news items of the day. The project began on January 1st 2012, but lasted just three months. Since then, some of the original poems were consigned to the bin; not fit for public consumption; the survivors being re-written to give them more accessibility going forward. Other poems were subsequently written of course, including some which were submitted as part of a collaboration with Fife artist, Joanna Foster for 'The Kingdom of If' arts project. So eventually, from the wreckage of such grand over ambitious beginnings, a collection did indeed emerge. I do hope you find something within these pages to enjoy; reflect upon and maybe even place next to your heart for safe keeping.

As always, I would like to thank the literary community within the North East of Scotland who have inspired and encouraged me in the last few years. It is a strong and vibrant scene and I don't believe you will find a better one anywhere in Scotland; maybe even within the UK! Thanks especially to **North East Writers, Pushing Out the Boat** magazine and the various bookshops and venues around the area that support us by hosting open poetry sessions; launches and readings (often for very little reward).

Finally thanks to my family for their encouragement and involvement; especially Joe for his proof reading skills and honesty in relation to the short stories.

Ellon - March 2013

Alien

walking, incongruous black

through dunes

re-planting marram grass

in clumps of poor argument

repeated, repeated, repeated

dull blades of rhetoric

blunted by the shifting sands

popular opinion is printed here

across the landscape

a wind driven, scouring har

but history and its stories

deep as the sand

wide as the water

are still chaired beside long winter fires

as dollars roar their demands

he does not hear

silence in decisions

or the grit of teeth

and at night

when dreams should dance

he counts himself

Anwar al-Balkimy

Anwar al-Balkimy

didn't like the nose he'd got

so he went to a clinic in Cairo

to cosmetically alter the blot

but later his nerve did a runner

and he up and surrendered his bed

then turned up again in a hospital

oh, he'd been robbed and beaten instead

now we all know about politicians

that the games they play can be nasty

but this one got caught with a hooter he'd bought

and Allah don't allow Rhinoplasty

As Christine Jorgensen

new star, a pause

lit between her lips

knife stylish

empty without love

knees together

nyloned, practiced

up to the job

pointless without a man

Marlene Dietrich

in her mind

she hears the fans

alone without them

smug telephone

black, silent

happy with itself

useless without words

checking the line again

she imagines a prince

gets the tone; no calls

nobody without calls

has the life

cashes it in for fame

trusts the cameras

history without the past

Aung San Suu Kyi

I feel the warmth of humanity

shifting quietly within my ears

a world whispering progress

a comfort of information

wrapping my heart in words

I am seen; observed and

protected by truth

unheard by some

unrecognised by others

I stand tall

in a field of dreams

in full view

of the world

Bad Samaritans

Two men posing as good Samaritans;
helped a young Malaysian student after
he'd been attacked during riots in London.
Then they robbed him.

there is fire

in the buildings

and people running,

running towards me now

at me

on me

then a fist

into my face

there is fire in my mouth

and I fall

good people help me

pick me up

say nice words

but wait

now they rob me

steal my things

what kind of

country is this?

Birth Prayer

A woman in north eastern Afghanistan

was arrested for allegedly murdering

her daughter-in-law, after she

gave birth to a third daughter.

my husband prays

it has to be a male child

my husband prays

his mother sits rocking in the next
room

it has to be a male child

my husband prays

his mother sits rocking in the next
room

even the flies around the bed mock me

it has to be a male child

my husband prays

his mother sits rocking in the next
room

even the flies around the bed mock me

the pain comes quickly now

it has to be a male child

my husband prays

his mother sits rocking in the next
room

even the flies around the bed mock me

the pain comes quickly now

it is done, the old midwife turns away

it has to be a male child

Blowing Cobwebs

walking the loch; the bidding laps

we squeeze mud into history

our footsteps whipping dew from grass

wetting boots and trouser drags

the wind thrills the water

throwing grey sky back to itself

and two swans bow;

approaching opportunities

geese scoot the rushing beds

combing our ears

into some straight talking

and the trees look on

Broken Drum

his mouth moves

with a beat I do not recognise

using percussion I do not understand

he looks human, but I want to

peel back his skin;

see what is inside his chest;

put out his eyes and

if I thought it would help

see inside his brain

does he drum with his head

or his heart; either way

I need to break his rhythm

as he broke mine

spill his blood;

being careful not to mix it

with the innocent dirt

under my feet

Bullets Never Rest

(December 14th 2012)

cars do not drive themselves

oceans do not float away to the stars

clouds still hide the moon

dogs remain at war with cats

steel does not bend easily

for the wind

buildings cannot speak

but, this one can today

in Newtown Connecticut

winter lives as

a glass echo in the trees

watching the waiting

flashing blue flowers

reflecting spasms of images

passing time

into a hopeless fall

quartet's of shoes

rooted in dance

are transfixed by

a crack in time

news comes as

a uniformed spectre

walking words

numb with repetition

reality twists

a blunt truth

as lives move across a screen

storm clouds gather

tears march to war

remembering

each face is a bullet and

bullets never rest

Bullied

they talk stone to me

sharp flinty words

shout sticks

barbed poles jabbed

at me, in the dark

they do not see

the stir of trouble

in my gut

the dirty wounds

inside my head

but they are there

they are there

now they are laughing

at me

around me

in me

I need to speak

my pain

to heal my wounds

Christchurch Cathedral

(February 2011)

Looking up at the sky

flooding new light

onto layers of prayer,

I try to draw up the words

from my gut.

Great lumping questions

that catch in my throat,

before falling

all the way to my knees

nailed to the floor.

There is silence here

but only the after silence

of roaring angels;

crashing wings in

dust and new light.

We will build new prayers

on blocks of hope;

out of the dust

and confusion

into the new light.

Cliff Edge

The renovation of a seventeenth century castle
near Cruden Bay in Aberdeenshire looked in
doubt when the developer failed to meet a deadline.
The castle is thought to have been the inspiration
behind Bram Stoker's Dracula!

you can't count on money these days
it washes in and out with the tide
floating on hope
rather than rafts of credit

blood sucking bankers
lose their teeth
chewing high stakes.
on the shore

even fine crashing views and
historical bricks
can't fill these purses

Colony

Zaag

yes Emperor

have the charges been set for destruction

yes Emperor

how long do we have

a quatrane of five

and what of earth

all is prepared

and the life forms

all zoned Emperor

the ruling ones

the ones that remain; Isolated

as requested

yes Emperor, in an area they call Antarctica

can they be integrated?

doubtful

then let them make of the land what they will

yes Emperor, you are most benevolent

yes Zaag

Dark Water

Everything is covered in a tailored white jacket. Here and there though hollows of black sulk against the sparkle of the hardening frost. It is a beautiful moonlit night across a scene I know well and I negotiate the densely overgrown shore with ease.

Lowering myself onto the trunk of a fallen tree, I pat it gently with my left hand. It's an old friend; the bark long shattered by years of highland weather. I trace the splitting grain with a finger, wondering how many years we have left together then raising my eyes, look through the shadow of a passing cloud and out across the loch. The dark waters shift and chop; playing disdainfully with the moon's reflection. After all these years, the loch still has its pride.

Behind me in the woodland, an owl calls out; arguing against the silence. I look over my shoulder into the trees, but after a moment I turn back to the loch and continue my search. Across the water, I can easily make out the slopes of the mountain crawling out of the gloom. Just over the other side of the summit, in a cleft between two massive granite cliffs, is our home. Well, it had been our home at one time. For many years now it had been a very exclusive holiday chalet for the few who could afford to buy its first class facilities (*and our memories*). At a thousand pounds a week, the views crashing against its stone façade, earn a fortune for the London businessman who is the

25

current owner. I always feel a detached resentment for anyone who stays there now.

A mixture of warm memories and cool regret, for something which can never be reclaimed washes over me; memories that somehow seem familiar and totally remote all at the same time. Rubbing my eyes firmly and refocusing my gaze onto the loch, I try to clear my head. It is nearly time and sure enough a moment later, as I stare at the surface of the water, it seems to slacken and quieten to a smoky mirror. Now I'm certain and I straighten my back.

A few seconds later, in the smoothest patch of water a few yards from the shore, something that appears to be the curve of a small leather football bobs into the moonlight and begins to move slowly and steadily towards me across the surface. The ball has an energy that seems to give it purpose and as it approaches the muddy shallows, it rises fully out of the water and becomes the head of a man; bald except for a small fringe of grey hair around the back. I recognise it immediately.

I stand up; begin to walk forward and in the clear blue black light I meet the gaze of my Father as he emerges from the loch.

Reaching the water's edge I offer him my hand and not taking his eyes from mine he grabs it with a cold, powerful grip. Reunited again we trudge back to the tree trunk. I steady him as he sits down and then easing away slightly join him, sitting astride the log so that I can see his profile. The loch drains slowly from him; glistening against the glow of the moon. We sit in silence for a few minutes. It is always a strange time for us; meeting again after another year; a year that feels like a thousand but, at the same time, like the single tick of a clock. After a while, he seems to relax a little and I speak.

"Well?"

The word is loaded in many ways and normally provokes a smile. But this time Father just looks tired; simply dropping his head slightly before slowly turning to look at me.

"It's no use. There's no sign of him anywhere." The words are heavy and only just manage to escape his lips.

I sigh deeply, but the cold damp air catches in my throat and I cough sharply.

"We must never give up, ever." I say eventually, letting my eyes wander again over the loch. "He's out there somewhere, I know he is."

Father watches me and then hangs his head again; slowly shaking it from side to side. "Why do we torture ourselves like this? It's time to go; time to join your Mother. If she can accept it, why can't we?"

"You know why. It's because we would never forgive ourselves, could not rest if we moved on and he was still in there, looking for us." My hand sweeps in an arc to show the size of the loch.

"You mean you wouldn't rest." he replies. Then adds wistfully, "Your Mother is at rest you know, together with Rosie and I think George is there as well! He's gone to be with them and here we are wondering around; two lost souls looking for the impossible."

In a way, I know he is right. We have searched nearly everywhere. But the thought of my young brother in the cold and dark depths of the loch, searching for us; searching for a light to guide him home when we have all deserted him, fills me with such a terrible fear, I know I have to go on. If eternity is something I have to give, I will give it, but I know Father is tired and wanting to be reunited with his wife; to have their eternity together at last. I can't deny him that, if that's what he needs

Moving along the tree trunk towards him, I take hold of one of his still damp hands and catch his eyes once more with mine, offering the smile that's been missing.

"You go and be with Mum; it's time. I'll carry on the search for a while just in case." Father's face softens and a small sad light flickers behind his eyes. "You must promise me one thing though." I continue, standing up. Father stands as well, "What's that?"

"If George is with Mum, you'll find some way of letting me know."

"I promise."

With that, he turns towards the water. Now that he is being released, time is of the essence.

"I'd better be off then." he says. "Don't be long, we'll all be waiting."

Suddenly I feel the need to embrace him; to exchange the one last thing that we have to share, in what is left of the darkness we have inhabited for so long, so I pull him gently to me and put my arms around him for a moment. As we part he looks into my eyes again, plucking the last ember of hope from within his soul and placing it in mine, then he turns and begins to walk away, towards the shore. Even before he has reached it though, I glimpse the water of the loch through his body, distorting his shape, absorbing him. In a second he is gone; two bodies dissolved into one.

I stand wondering what it might feel like. Maybe I will never know.

What I do know is that all of a sudden I feel more alone than ever. Perhaps it's that feeling that will keep me going. Maybe I'll need that pain to remind myself in the future; why I let Father go at last and why I hadn't gone with him.

Sitting down, I reach into my jacket pocket and pull out a sodden piece of paper. A clipping from a newspaper I had found, abandoned on the shore, twenty three years before. Unfolding it delicately, I spread it out on the wood beside me and gaze at it sadly.

The words scream up at me from the paper, as I relive the events of that day and how we came to lose George. The report lists our names, ages, where we'd once lived and how and where the wreck of our boat had been found. It speculates about the cause, but only we know what really happened! The images, the noise and surprisingly the smell and taste of terror as our boat was smashed to pieces by something unseen in the fog, would be stitched onto our souls forever.

Spears of sunlight are beginning to shatter the cold air, as I rise from my resting place for the last time; folding and returning the clipping to my pocket. I walk to the muddy shoreline, pausing only briefly before wading in and as the icy water claws its way up my body, a reflex, learned long ago, begs me to take a breath but instead, I lift my head to greet the loch.

"Hold on George, I'm coming for you...hold on."

End

Davey

hey hey we were

Saturday morning pictures

rowdy cartoon kids

rainy home holidays

muddy knees

playground chatter boxes

TV dreamers

swinging sick school days

Smash Hits blankets

Woolworth loiterers

singing impressionists

late Sunday breakfasts

pyjamas on toast

hey hey

we were The Monkees

Debrief

I once tried to interrogate

a broken heart on its injuries

sit it down in its chest

at first it didn't speak

or even acknowledge me

in my black cloak

so I swallowed

my questions

deep inside a smile

it then thanked me

for showing compassion

(you know)

after everything

I told it not to worry

but could feel

the warmth of its defeat

Defacement

what of paint

does it argue the point

reason

defend a different

point of view

ask questions

does it listen

understand

accept

believe

what of paint

does it endure

beyond a colour

if so, then

what of steel

Dissection

'Tell me who invented the human heart and

then show me the place where he was hanged.'

Lawrence Durrell – The Alexandria Quartet (Justine)

It is early morning and the sun is only just beginning to strip the moisture from the damp Paris streets. I am thinking about love.

The pavement café is deserted as I ask the waiter poised beside me for just a plate and a sharp knife to accompany my espresso.

I recognise him from when we'd eaten here a few days ago; my wife had loved his French accent. I'd noticed the way he looked at her and watched her as she gazed up at him while he took our order. The light in her eyes and the way she held her mouth; slightly open with the tip of her tongue resting just between her lips, had made me want to leave there and then, but something had held back me in a sort of voyeuristic trance. She wanted to come to Paris, because she thought it was the capital of romance; the heart of love. She thought all French men talked liked David Ginola, the footballer. Watching her then, with the waiter, I'd felt like a hunter waiting for the perfect shot.

The waiter responds with a raised eyebrow and a quick glance at the menu, as if to check whether my request appears as a side order. Then he peers down, around the edge of the table to the carrier bag at my feet, presumably to see if I have some food of my own tucked inside. He raises his hand to his mouth, coughs and smiles weakly, then gestures at the sign on the wall which states quite clearly, that only food purchased at the cafe can be consumed on the premises. I smile back and ask for a croissant, insisting though that he provide a sharp knife so that I can cut it. This makes him frown with contempt, but scribbling in his notebook he heads inside. As my eyes follow him I notice the sharp creases in his shiny black trousers and the crispness of his white shirt; deciding that he is just too neat for his own good. Someone someday would take great delight in messing him up.

My thoughts continue on love, as I watch the pigeons fluttering around the square like windblown leaves. As they copulate; rattling and beating their wings, I wonder if there is one split second, within their miserable little lives when they experience any feeling that would be recognised as love. They have hearts, I know that, but I doubt that they love with them. I wonder if I should pity them this lack of emotion; or envy them *(is ignorance bliss?)*. In drifting moments; when I am reluctant to grant love a place in my life, I often find myself looking inwards at my own heart; much like a parent constantly checks a child to see if it is alright; to see if it is awake. I then begin to wonder if hearts have anything to do with love at all.

Maybe love is held only by the ones that feel loved and those that believe they love (*heart's of the unloved are therefore lost*). I'm reminded that at times, to me, love feels like some sort of dangerous dance floor, with my heart the one solitary dancer - at the mercy of myself! Maybe love is something we are all ensnared in while we wait for death; like life tricking our hearts into entering a darkened room, locking the door and snapping the key. That image scares me, so I try to forget love for a while; internally discussing other subjects in great detail, to the exclusion of everything else. Suddenly I realise that I'm thinking about it again; it's like rain falling on sodden ground and Robert Plant starts singing in my head:

'If it keeps on raining, the levee's going to break and when

the levee breaks, I'll have no place to stay'.

Sitting back in my chair and laying my hands palm down on the table, I start to hold my breath for as long as I can; trying to starve my brain of oxygen so that it can't think anymore.

I give up a few seconds later when the waiter arrives with my order. No knife! I sigh, thinking that it would have been much easier to have brought one with me! I look up at him and raise an eyebrow in what I hope is enough of a question for him. He raises an eyebrow in reply, nods his head curtly and turns away with just enough implied impertinence, in order to greet an elderly couple who are just walking in. They are dressed smartly as if attending a formal function. If they had been younger I might have guessed that they were returning home after an all night party; but then again I cannot tell how old their hearts are so...

The waiter seats them in the corner; about as far as possible from me it would seem, but it is so quiet I can still hear them as they place their order. They ask him for coffee and croissants and he once again returns to the kitchen (*where does his heart lie and with whom?*). As the lady removes her leather gloves, I steal a look at her left hand. An expensive looking solitaire diamond tries to impress me across the tables, but the solid band of gold next to it denies its brilliance.

'Ah, real love.' I whisper to myself.

On the table next to me are the remains of a partially eaten meal. A plate that seems to have once contained a breakfast of eggs and some sort of fatty meat lies rejected, with a neatly mated knife and fork sleeping together in the debris. Next to it is an empty coffee cup; some of its former contents dribbled down one side; just below a neatly printed crescent of pink lip gloss. I try to visualise the lips that had sipped the hot liquid from the rim of the cup, but cannot without falling in love with the image in my head (*for such a small device a heart, it would seem, is such a big open space to fill*). I reach over and carefully pluck the knife from the plate before the waiter returns. Even so, I get a puzzled look from the elderly gentleman who is looking at me over his wife's shoulder. He mutters something quietly to her; half shielding his mouth with his hand. She turns to look in my direction, but only raises her eyes at the last moment and just for a split second, as if she is afraid to catch my eye. She turns back to her husband and the back of her neck flushes above her orange silk scarf.

I close my eyes for a moment; simplifying the world in the blink of an eye and when I re-open them, I am turning the knife over and over in my hand, seeing the reflections of everything around me twisted in its blade. My mouth corrupts a smile as I return it to the table and reach down to lift the carrier bag from the floor onto my lap. Inside the bag my hand closes on another smaller plastic bag; tied at the top with a simple knot. I'm not sure if it's the excitement of beginnings, or a fear of endings that make my fingers tremble as they untie the knot and slip inside. I tenderly grip the heart and pull it slowly from the bag, placing it on the plate in front of me. Even as it settles onto the white porcelain, it is shouting questions so loudly that my head cannot hear them (*what...who...where...how?*).

But, for the answers, I need to act quickly. I snatch the knife up again and as I bend to my task, exerting pressure with the sharp blade, a small drop of crimson escapes with a sigh onto the white linen tablecloth. I smile at the fatal irony as I realise that this heart, the bluntest of objects, has cut me as surely as the blade now slicing across its flesh. I continue to slash hurriedly through the seeping organ, pulling at its valves and chambers with the fingers of my other hand; desperately searching for answers, until it lies flat and deflated on the plate.

'Nothing, nothing but lies. You bitch!' I shout, as a crimson delta of blood creeps away across the table cloth; escaping its life sentence (*love always runs away*). The remains look exhausted and empty; unrecognisable and shrunken like the corpse of an old dead friend (*what have I done?*). I recognise it now as my own heart, here in front of me, dead and without any hope of salvation as if I had torn it from my own body. I am aware of the elderly gentleman calling for the waiter in a strangled, gulping voice. I cannot hear his companion; so I assume she is busy somewhere finding a scream to fill her throat. I grip the handle of the knife now with both hands and turning the blade to point at myself, I begin to push its tip into my chest. There is a brief moment of pain as the knife reaches the skin beneath my clothes, when suddenly my head snaps to the right and my chair rocks madly on its legs; almost toppling over. The knife is thrown from my grip and clatters onto the floor. Gasping for air, I raise my hand to my left cheek that is stinging with a sharp heat. Something or someone had struck my face.

My eyes click open and I look up to see the waiter, who appears to be a little less neat and composed than earlier, standing over me. He is looking at me with a concerned and frightened expression; the elderly couple are looking on just behind him. Her face is crimson (*blood*); his is grey and wrapped in a stiffening cloak of disdain. I see that he is holding a mobile telephone to his ear and is speaking to someone using deep spittled words that I cannot make out. Then I slump in the chair, staring at the table, where the croissant lies on the plate, chopped

39

up into small jagged pieces; shards scattered across the cloth.

The waiter is still looking at me, but his expression is already changing from concern to pity as he tells me I must be feeling unwell; suggesting that I wait for the doctor that has been called. I try to reply, but even I know that my words are not making any sense, so I hurriedly stand and throwing a twenty euro note onto the table, grab the carrier bag from the floor before muttering a weak apology. I stagger from the café and across the road; running erratically off down the nearest street and through the gathering rush hour.

-o-

As I thread my way through the crowds on the left bank of the river, I catch sight of a beautiful young girl; Paris slim with auburn hair, dressed in the tightest of light blue denim jeans and a tan leather flying jacket. She stops beside an artist who is painting and speaks to him. They laugh at something he says and she tidies a strand of unruly hair behind her right ear.

I sit down on a bench that overlooks the river, observing them for a while as they talk and laugh together. A stray dog that has been sniffing around a nearby rubbish bin, trots over to the bench and takes a great deal of interest in the carrier bag beside me. I push the dog away roughly and it circles the bench looking intently at the bag, then at me and then back to the bag, before lying down next to a tree across the path.

I look back to the girl and her friend who are still talking and laughing; obviously love is no challenge for them. Eventually they part; exchanging kisses on each other's cheeks. She walks in my direction and I cannot help but stare at her face; my tongue resting just between my open lips. As she approaches the bench where I'm sitting, she glances across and smiles gently at me; an open, innocent *(inviting)* smile and even though I don't know her, I can see she has a warm heart. Maybe she has just enough love left for me.

I stand up as she is about to pass by and turning my head towards her, wish her a good morning. She pauses to look at me, raising one eyebrow in cautious enquiry and I realise that she's even prettier close up; her lightly tanned face looks as if it's been sculptured; her jaw and cheeks smooth and unblemished.

"Good morning, Monsieur." She replies in English, seeing through my inadequate French accent. "Can I help you in any way; are you lost?"

I instantly panic as I have no real reason to talk to her, beyond an inexplicable impulse and I stammer madly, searching for an idea. I suddenly feel very warm and uncomfortable and unzip my jacket, at which point she look down; her eyes widening as if she suddenly understands. She lays a hand delicately on my arm.

"Ah Monsieur, do you require a hospital, perhaps?" I'm taken aback and shake my head slowly.

"But Monsieur, votre chemise...your shirt, look!" I follow her gaze which is fixed upon my chest and see the smattering of dried, dark red stains and smudges across my shirt front. My mind starts to whirl in confusion and I stumble a few paces backwards, dropping the carrier bag and falling to the ground. I pull the jacket around me, mumbling stupidly. The girl, stretching out her hand, seems concerned for a moment and takes a step forward, but thinking better of it turns on her elegant heels and with a single backwards glance, hurries off along the path. I wait for a minute, watching her walk off and then, slowly getting to my feet, follow her along the path, leaving the carrier bag lying on the ground.

-o-

The stray dog rises from its resting place by the tree, saunters across to the bag and begins to nuzzle it gently. Encouraged by what it can smell, it begins to rip at the bag, to get to the contents. Some children run by; excitedly chasing a kite flown by one of the group. The dog lifts its head to watch them pass, licking its nose.

End

Do you remember?

Dear Mum,

You're probably trying to guess where I am. Well this letter won't tell you where I am, but it will tell you why I've gone.

Do you remember a few weeks ago, when you were in the greenhouse and I came in to ask you about my homework and we started talking about how I was doing at school? Do you remember?

Can you remember what we talked about? Probably not, because I know that you were busy; especially with Jamie's chickenpox and Dad being away on his golfing trip and everything else; I do understand. Well, along with the usual things, like lessons and how I was getting on with the new teacher, we talked about Paul Hilliard and how he and Steven Page had beaten me up in the locker room after football. Do you remember?

You said I should ignore them and they'd go away, well they didn't and I wasn't surprised really because they had been on my case for quite a long time and looking the other way while one of them sat on my chest doing 'the typewriter' was never going to work, ever! Apart from that, they were really clever and always picked on me when nobody else was about and then when we were in class they always sucked up to the teachers, so I was never going to be believed, even if I had dobbed them in.

Do you remember last Friday, when I came home late from school and my uniform was muddy and you told me off for mucking about and grounded me for the weekend? That was them; they were waiting for me up the road. In the last few days they'd broken my mobile and robbed me of my dinner money, saying that I had to bring them more or they would really hurt me. On Sunday, you said I was a bit quiet and you probably thought it was just me sulking because I had been told off. It wasn't that, it was because it was nearly Monday and I'd have to face them again.

I've got to go now. Sorry but I needed some money, so I've taken some from the jar in the kitchen cupboard. Give my love to Dad and Jamie.

Do you remember when we went to the zoo last year? We had a good time didn't we, except for when I was sick after eating too much ice cream. Do you remember?

Love Josh x

Doing Time

my fear is a grey blanket

anonymous, blending, invisible

hate on my face

is my body language

constant, hard, unmoveable

I hide pain behind my eyes

strong, unemotional, steady

cover loathing with a smile

convincing, practiced, necessary

my faith is with all gods and all men

devout, humble, active

preserving trust in memories

past, present and future

Double Step Whilst Smiling

During the pasodoble

I detect a hint of carnivore

about you that

sustains my nausea.

Is it an echo

of disobedience

or the scent

of glossed over excuses

that wiggles its finger

through the bars of

your allure?

These are brief customs of bliss

they are your dances

therefore

they are ours.

Elephant in the City

at the lips of the swallowing city

the sun pushes aside a grip of trees

benches slit cold light to the concrete

and sticky spits

amongst a million chatted dogs

seagulls swipe at unwrapping overnighters

a fresh coffee bruise spilled onto the old

a one hundred and forty million pound

January morning on Union Plaza

Elizabeth II

a loss delivered

within a conversation of arms

to a straightening back and

four walls

a young woman and

a door

leading to

a life as Queen

and neither her

dutiful eyes

or her heart

have ever darkened

Ellon

we came to Ellon;
finally found it
hidden in the trees
called it home

this island town
a crossing place
for reflections

we kissed against
the surprising sea;
the full bodied land and
flowing water

the meandering sky
blood lined
along the river

Empty Pews

the church doors stand open

inside, the pews march

down the nave

altarbating

shoving love back

at Christ's feet;

not needed anymore

the pews chant:

"We have our own

carpenter now;

we are carved

in our own image."

stoutly, solidly

the doors slam shut;

echoing congregations

Extremist

you kick the sun

grab the fractured light

in your hand

punch the wind

embrace the twisted breeze

with your arms

stab the sea

slicing it into thin puddles

with your tongue

shoot the sky

feel its blood fall

onto your tilted face

you load a gun

with ideals

and watch the death

of innocents

Fingal's Cave

love cannot be found

more solid than this

existence more telling

hidden in a tomb of storms

a cave of words

each letter thought into rock and

declared as rough edged

permanent emotion

what a pact they brokered

with history

what faith in

failing waves

Five Years of Hope

The body of British hostage, Alan McMenemy
was handed into the British Embassy in Baghdad;
five years after he was kidnapped whilst on duty
as a security guard.

how far can hope stretch

for years

as far as a wish

for a lifetime

as long as love

for eternity

until uncertainty snaps

five years

is enough

for anyone

Fred the Shred

Fred the Shred is over drawn, at the cash point of excuses

he's been found out and lost his clout, for his RBS abuses

his knighthood has been debited; he's a sad disgraced ex-banker

he's not Sir Freddie anymore; he's just a silly wanker.

Yes, Mr Goodwin's in the club with Mugabe and Ceausescu

his social standing's gone to pot, too late to mount a rescue

the made to measure suit of steel, he used to polish proudly

has lost its shine, it's gone all dull; his sunny life's gone cloudy.

The charger that he rode upon, when he risked financial ruin

is no longer on the battlefield, but in a tin and used for gluing

so Fred the Shred is now retired; just a man for the press to pester

and the controversial banking post, is filled by 'Uncle Fester'!

Gabrielle

a bullet in a woman's head

thinks its work is done and retires

a woman stands and fights

the sun, the moon and the whole

damn universe

a madman fails to stand and

justice lets him sleep

pushing his knees into his chest

a woman grows to the size

of Arizona and six souls smile

Gene Variant

it doesn't take a genius

to see that you like cream

stuff more cake inside your mouth

go on, make sure your plate is clean

and when the buttons on your shirt

spin off in all directions

you can always blame biology

for your confectionary affections

Guantanamo 1

Time

ticking clock hammer

I hear it somewhere

in this room

it strikes in the counting

of hairs on my arm

the pores of my skin

bricks, holes in bricks

holes in the holes

a pin prick universe.

Guantanamo 2

Time

infinite piercing blade

with no point to soften the blow

no hilt to stop the thrust

a wound of

dreaming windows

open doors

pathways with no end

horizons unreached

unfound.

Haiku

shopping on rails

tipping tins into trolleys

re-stocking life

with wallets

-o-

six foot two in a hoodie

average height in a navy tracksuit

two men?

-o-

headmaster gets his pupils caught

in carpet versus shoe debacle

-o-

open your eyes

blood on the wall

should tell you to stop

banging your head

-o-

puddle on a December road

a grey retirement home

for snowflakes

-o-

on Mondays

newsagents kiss the golden coins

on the paperboy's eyes

-o-

she wears a duster for a skirt and

everyday crawls over men to work

Hello Daddy

PLAY>

Her voice is a spirit,

a warmth in the room

sucking memories

out of thin air and

injecting them straight

into my heart.

I listen and listen,

replaying missed inflections

paraphrasing every sentence

in my head.

I am sipping a delicate infusion,

deconstructing a complex dish

on the back of my tongue,

allowing tastes and aromas to

settle the stomach of memories

before rewinding again.

PLAY>

Home to Roost

all those years of feather plucking

wishbone pulls

and chestnut stuffing

all that gravy

made for nothing

the turkey's home to roost

all those plates of leg and breast

carving knives

and shirt fronts messed

all the family

over dressed

the turkey's home to roost

all those scraps wrapped up in paper

doggy bags

cold cuts for later

for Jesus Christ?

we forgot to cater

the turkey's home to roost

House of Horror

Hammer studios issued a public appeal

for footage, cut from some of their films

by the censors.

am   ated

   put

   apitated

dec

disem   led

        bowel

dis   ed

   member

I.E.D.

hot air punches diagonals

everything falls slowly

screaming for the dust

to settle   *(left arm missing)*

already sticky in the heat

the flow of life

welds blood to the sand

a darker camouflage

hand grips sand

love binds love

in the flooding light

pressed into the wall

a ring

gold and commitment

IC R1646

a safe pair of hands

Mr Brown

gossamer memories

carried like prayers

from the gathering

hillside and January snow

eight answers

twisted from the metal

delivered to gods and

seventy years on

still safe

Impatient Ignorance

I need an explanation

of how and why.

When it will all

begin to make sense?

I hear you; stay close.

I will now ask you a question

about everything.

I need a quick answer and

preferably as a one

word thesis.

Isolation

fear and anger

turn feet into walls

twist mouths into wire

stuff hands into pockets

glue eyes to floors

like jealous twins

they never smile

never listen

only believe

in themselves

Jail Fire

mothers, smelling death

gather in the street

join twisted hands

in low moans of prayer

imagine the blackness

which is

worse than knowing

shadows on shadows

layers of many screams

scratched onto dust

echoes in the soot

unheard shouts in the smoke

useless fists in the flames

no defence

a parade of body bags

float out of the main gate

into the waiting ambulances

and freedom

Keepin' Alive

Does anyone know any Bee Gees' hits

a man kneeling beside a body

New York Mining Disaster 1941

a woman in the crowd

How does it go

Not sure

Does it have a good beat

Can't remember

How about, Night Fever

a middle aged man

Something like that

God I wish I could remember

How about the kiss of life

the woman again

Was it in Saturday Night Fever

How Deep is Your Love – Jive Talking

a chorus from the crowd

I know... Stayin' Alive

a voice from the back

My favourite

the body on the ground

Lies Shot in the Dark

(Paul Carter)

a family folded

in the dark

a secret folded

in the dark

a truth folded

in the dark

a lie folded

in the dark

a file folded

in the dark

a life folded

in the dark

Long Blue

(beachcombing 1)

the ocean whispers

frothy moon journeys

dripping sunsets and

thin blue lines

roars

twisted metal

shattered wood and

long blue lives

Meaning?

is it Gods that speak

or devils

when men take up arms

against fellow men

is it bombs and guns

which preach now

from pulpits of torn bodies

and burning cars

is there no

word for meaning

any more

no word for love

is devoutness

a barricade

an unpainted corner

on a floor of ideals

is...?

Mending a Net

(beachcombing 2)

tooled by tides

turned and turned

by strong fingers

on big heart hands

working hard

weaving thoughts

into stitches

spinning tales

onto the quay

and always

a flicker of eyes

a cracked smile

just for me

Missing Person

nothing

is too deep a place to go

even for thought, even

to fetch a silent hope

it would be a reach too far

like black falling down

a hard stretch

someone has cut his wire

stepped into a burst bubble

with a blind roar

leaving an empty chair

and a room in silence

disappeared

gone missing

Like Moths

their words, like moths

are heard

in the dark

behind a powder wall

survive briefly

then get burned

under the spotlight

and flapping

fall on deafened ears

Mugabe's Heart

outside the presidential palace

in the dust

the beggars play

pass the parcel

with a ball

of blood soaked newspaper

they smile

happy in their game

My Twist of the Knife

my body opened the door

to a stranger; invited it in

I did not welcome it

offer it tea and biscuits, or a seat even

but there it was having lunch in my womb

that made me mad

I hadn't prepared for a guest

certainly not an overnighter

or longer and in my bed too

nothing was clear; nothing was clean

it had to go

five weeks later I was ready

its bags were packed and in the porch

my hand was turning the key

when it turned and smiled

stuffing my heart into my throat

choking me

making the biggest swallow of my life

it was Mother, Father,

me in black and white

one for the album

my own twist of the knife

Nanny's State

Nanny says:

you will eat well

and healthily.

She has recipes for you

that will only cost five pounds

to make and

if Ainsley Harriott can do it

anyone can.

The best bit is,

your local supermarket

will help by

selling you all the ingredients

you'll need

for less than Nanny thinks

you can afford.

Visit Ainsley's tutorial

on the website;

he'll show you how.

See Nanny's leaflet for details.

Newborn

if we smile,

touch hands, if

just for a moment

we make eye contact

with each other,

we may both laugh,

cry, even feel a little fear

but then

we will love

One Hundred and One

In a trial at the Old Bailey, a couple were accused of inflicting one hundred and one wounds on a fifteen year old boy using sticks and a metal bar along with other tools; because they believed he was a witch. The boy, Kristy Bamu died of his injuries.

newham 2010

one hundred and one

a new number

of the beast

one hundred and one

a number of ways

to deny something

one hundred and one

a number of wounds

to prove nothing

one hundred and one

a number of ways

to cry

Orbit

Former astronaut and Senator John Glenn celebrated the fiftieth anniversary of his Earth orbit by chatting with the crew on the International Space Station. Glenn was the first man to orbit the earth in February 1962.

1962

we start the future here

in the present

and there

in our ambition

where we fly friendship and

stars hang on every word

of our hope

2012

the future was started there

in the past

and here

in the present

where we now fly memories and

hope hangs on

every star of our words

Parking Progress

Aberdeenshire council introduced a cashless parking scheme in Stonehaven, despite virtually no backing from residents.

Notice:

everyone has a mobile phone

these days, apparently

there's a societal trend

towards technology and

anyway, as we're

expecting a new wave

of twenty-somethings

to come through soon,

it's bound to catch on

so, anyone over the age of fifty

found trying to use

these parking facilities

by force feeding

loose change into

a passing scaffie

will have their cars confiscated

and re-cycled

into mobility scooters

Pax

*In Yemen; a few weeks before he was supposed to resign and
leave the country, president Ali Abdullah Saleh passed a law
granting immunity to himself and anyone who served under him
from prosecution for crimes against protesters involved in a
recent uprising.*

you can

be held responsible

for the beatings

the shooting of

your people

in the streets

you have

done bad things

your fingers

might be crossed

behind

your backs

but that is real

blood on your heels

as you walk

away

Pit

(Hester pit disaster 1862)

every miner and his family knew

the fresh steps down the Hester and

black stepped return

that ticked the time each day

the single shafted route to pay

as toil it served as toil

but mouths craved the food it bought, so

down they had to go

until death sang their song

with a roar

dust could not carry life

to those left at the top

and as a fresh field waited

so did tables

for bread

Planting Futures

new year's day

at the edge of the world

the sea recounts its stories

of past shores

to the fractured, footed sand

sighs to the sloping ears

of dogged walkers

everywhere is gold

that will not shade

to yellow or brown

the sun drifts lower

picking jewels from the waterline

freeing ghosts from the waves

bewildered by horizons

half lit faces gaze

along the dunes

planting futures there

Preacher

It is rarely sandal weather

on Inverness High Street

even in the summer

the wind can bite.

Thin cotton robes

are not Harris Tweed

or Berghaus and

this is February.

A man on a corner shouts

sharp fractured words

into a microphone

a blind man's highland frost.

People look the other way, or

check mobile phones

I do not recognise the words

the man does not recognise me.

Punishment

The room was quiet and cold as Duncan bent down and reached beneath the floorboards. Resting in the dust between the joists was a small box which he lifted out and placed onto the floor. Looking up for a moment, he watched the dust that was streaming in through the window, dance in the sunlight.

He winced as he looked down again at the box and recognising the sharp ache that was settling behind his eyes, rested his hands gently against the box for a moment, until the pain subsided. The box felt warm as if someone had, just moments before, been holding it exactly as he was doing now. It was about six inches square and four inches deep, was made of light coloured wood and plain, except for a circle of silver metal, inlaid into the surface around the keyhole. The joint between base and lid was perfect; the work of a craftsman. Without thinking, he tried to open the box. It was locked, but of course he knew that.

The headache that had been brewing suddenly intensified, making him wince again and he closed his eyes for a moment. When Duncan opened them again, he was looking at the key, next to where the box had been lying. Bending forward, he picked it up and inserted it into the keyhole. He felt and heard a satisfying click as the key turned. The lid opened smoothly. The inside of the box was also plain, with no lining and sitting in the bottom, was a white envelope. Duncan whispered "Nearly there Babe." and as soon as the words drifted from his lips, the headache eased. He smiled gently, looked briefly up towards the cracked, flaking ceiling, and winked.

The envelope was in his hands now and turning it over, he slid one of his fingers under the flap, opening it slowly. Inside was a folded sheet of writing paper and two small photographs. Keeping hold of the paper, Duncan put the snaps down onto the floor and stared down at them. They had been taken during a trip to London, not long after they'd met and as he looked at them, a feeling of longing stabbed at his heart. There was Jane, on a bench at Victoria railway station, looking up at him with her beautiful smile and in the other photograph, next to her on another bench there he was, grinning stupidly in front of St Paul's Cathedral. Stupid was ok though, he thought to himself; after all it's what love does to you.

Unfolding the paper, he looked at the words written there; words written in his own, rather scruffy hand. He knew what they said of course, but he read them silently to himself again anyway; as he always had to. Reading them always filled him with a complex mixture of feelings; none of which he could explain; leastways not after all these years. He could explain the tears though, that had begun to creep out from behind his eyes.

Duncan hung his head and let them come and as he did so he knew Jane was there now, sitting in the corner by the window, watching him. The light was fading a little now, but it didn't matter, she carried her own light with her, within her own image. He blinked, trying to clear away the tears and looked up.

"Hello, Duncan"

"Hi, Babe"

"You made it then?"

"When have I ever let you down?"

Jane held his gaze for a moment and then looked towards the window without answering. Eventually she turned back to him.

"My heart is such a dark place these days, I'm not sure what to expect anymore; but it feels so much lighter again when we're together. I think that somehow we must create a sort of energy field between us."

"It's why we're here babe."

They remained in silence for a minute. It was nice to be together again, even though they knew in reality, they could never truly be together again. It was Duncan who broke the silence.

"I wish I could hold you again"

"Don't"

"Sorry, I know we can't, it's just that I wish somehow that this would end and we could be together properly forever. It's just not fair"

"Fairness is reserved for the living Duncan, remember?"

Duncan sighed, "But they will find us one day wont they?"

"Maybe, but if I'm honest they're probably not looking anymore."

He knew she was right and together they lapsed into silence again; submerged within their own thoughts.

The long periods of silence were normal, but eventually Duncan let out a deep sigh and asked the question they both had been holding onto, deep within their souls, for a long time.

"Were we right, Babe; to do...what we did?"

Jane, who had been peering out of the window as if she were looking or waiting for something, turned towards him. She was crying.

"I just don't know now; I've been thinking the same thing, over and over. I suppose we should ask ourselves whether we're happier; if the answer's no, then no, I don't think we were right."

"I'm happy at the moment."

"So am I," she sobbed, realising the irony of her words, "But is this moment enough? Is it worth suffering the eternal blackness, just for these few moments together each year? If only they'd found the box and the letter, before they left the house!"

"They were punishing us...f!"

"What?"

"They were punishing us...for leaving *them*; for not being...there...anymore." Duncan stuttered over his words. "The thing is, I'm not sure if this, or the...darkness is the punishment! Either way, I think we're dammed! I can't stand being apart, but this is almost as bad; knowing that we've only a short time together before..." Duncan's voice trailed off as he fought with what was left of his emotions.

"I know." replied Jane. "I think we both know, Duncan."

In their hearts, the one thing that neither of them could know was when, or if this punishment would ever end. The short moments together in what was left of the old house were the only thing they had a measure of control over; were the only things remaining that seemed real to them. For the time being this was life, of a sort. It somehow encapsulated their love; held it safe, but unlike the box that now sat between them on the floor, the place that held their love had no key; could not be opened to set them free.

It was nearly time to go. Duncan placed the photos and the letter back in the box, locked it and replaced it back under the floorboards with the key. He looked over to Jane and although the room was dark now, Duncan could just see the pattern of the faded wallpaper leaking through her slowly fading body.

"Babe?"

She turned her head and looked across at Duncan, smiling gently despite her sadness. "I know; I can see the light switch through your head!"

Duncan smiled back, bending down to replace the boards he'd taken up. He would have to move quickly; in a few minutes he would not be able to touch, or pick up anything.

It took just a moment to replace the boards back into place and as he worked, Duncan kept glancing over at Jane. Pushing the last piece of wood into place, he rose to his feet. Jane was also standing now; barely visible in the corner.

"Time to go Babe."

"I know, goodbye Duncan. Keep wishing my darling."

"I will. I miss you so much."

"I miss you too."

With that, the room was empty again and as quiet as any grave. Very quickly, even the fabric of the room; the walls, the floor and the ceiling, all began to fade. The outside began to drift inside, like air invading a vacuum. Eventually, where once had stood brick, tile, lathe and plaster, wood and glass, there was just a simple shroud of damp, neatly cut turf and nothing above it but the night sky.

End

Rain

Over one thousand prisoners in Kyrgyzstan jails sewed their lips together as part of an ongoing protest against continued beatings. The lips were stitched in such a way as to allow the consumption of fluids but not food.

they beat us like rain

the bruises soaking our skin

but not our souls

we sew our mouths shut

they will save money on food

and if we continue

they will save water as well

they beat us like rain, but

we will drink the rain

Raoul Moat's Last Victim

opening my eyes

each morning

I see darkness

see bad men

haunting me

running me

shaping a man

but see less

of a man

I feel my way

in the dark

touch sharp surfaces

unnatural edges

unfamiliar feelings

clutch for

all the strings

I once held

that are

no longer there

opening my eyes

each morning

I see darkness

Renegade

sipping coffee

thinking

smoking a cigarette

dreaming

ironing a shirt

writing a letter

shooting innocent people

including children and dragging

their bodies into one room

before burning them

playing solitaire

cutting yourself shaving

eating a burger

masturbating

composing a suicide note

Return as Sand

American businessman, Donald Trump said he would halt work on his new golf resort at Menie, if ministers grant permission for the installation of eleven wind turbines in Aberdeen bay.

the sea will rise and fall each day

a wind will blow onto or off of the land

grass will bend, but will not break

sand will shift as opinion shifts

from place to place

then return as sand

judges will preach to the sky and

expect it to listen

they may wave

their arms for ever but

there is no law here but the sky

and only the sky

Fire Risk

A woman out on a hen night suffered burns, after candles on a nearby table set fire to the toilet roll wedding dress she was wearing.

if your dress is made of Andrex

and you're going out at night

just beware of any naked flames

that could set your frills alight

be careful on the dance floor to, if

you're wearing three ply tissue

make sure there's an extinguisher close at hand

when fire becomes an issue, also

don't be tempted to dress in Izal,

cos it's shiny and it's scratchy

and its fire retardant character

is best described as patchy

so think of health and safety eh?

and forget the bog roll couture

your fashion won't be as flammable and

you'll look less like a freak, that's for sure

Rubbish

Images of the rubbish filled flat in Paisley released by the Crown Office, show where a two year old was murdered by his mother. She kept the death of her son a secret from friends and family for several months.

beer can cuddle

milk bottle hunger

crisp packet cries

juice bottle cough

tin can sores

newspaper fever

carrier bag mother

disposable love

rubbish life

Salt Window

(beachcombing 3)

sauce bottle bottom

catching the sun

a disc, passed a shine

normality etched

by sand and sea

netted memories of

a family meal

steamed voices

through a salt window

Sand Fire

(beachcombing 4)

we gathered tree bones

beached, bleached

laid them

stacked them

crossed them together and

touching a flame

made a pyre

against night chills

we smoked words

toasted tall stories

curled toes in the cold sand

wind tugged sparks

flying as dreams

Seal

(beachcombing 5)

hauled out

played out

basking on shingle

a given name

that has no memory

of itself

faded, forgotten in

swirling ceramic seas

just a seal,

selkie

or toy

oh but what pictures

of play

She's Holding On

tottering on pavements

no-body clears anymore

woollen stockings, sensible shoes

small steps;

not even strides

at the kerb, she's holding on

between the cars

stuck for days in the snow

mumbled shuffling words

agreeing with her feet

across the road now

pausing for clouds to pass

heaving inside the strain

of her old coat;

too small since babies

setting off again

shopping bag scrapping

whispers in the ice

in search of tatties,

for soup

a mutter of wishes

steaming her progress

a condensation of prayers

on her cheeks; few answered

she's holding on

at the grocery van

purse exhausted, flattened again

a pocket of holes

takes her hand

wishing her a merry Christmas

heavy bag homeward

messages rush by

playing back soup and

warm hearths

in her memory head

misjudging the traffic

all her years fall

to a rubber scream and

a hand reaching down.

she's holding on

Shifting Silver

*The Captive Animals' Protection Society claimed that the
Scottish Government spent nearly £48,000 on a party for two
giant panda's, when they arrived from China, on lease to
Edinburgh zoo.*

an unusual ornament

a syrup tin

a mantelpiece condiment

for rainy days

and tight belts

where every day

wears a coat

a birthday

a shiny bottomed dip and

disappointment

no party for the bairns

no shifting silver for mum

just gold for the man and

Pandas for the zoo

Slave

An orphaned girl from Pakistan told a court in Greater Manchester about her ordeal at the hands of an elderly couple. The girl was beaten, raped and forced to work for nothing during the day and sleep on a concrete floor in a locked cellar at night.

my life

cold the floor, hard the bones

my body

aching the flesh, hot the bruises

despair is praying, hoping a

leather stride of denials

sweat and blood, a weight of hate

my life

cold the memories, hard the future

my body

hot the scars, aching the muscles

waking is working, sleeping a

metal scrape of dreams

keys and locks, a chain of pain

Slow Moving Line

*Scientists discovered the genetic footprint of a giant tortoise
species, thought to have been extinct for 150 years, in the
DNA of 84 tortoises in the Galapagos Islands; suggesting that
pure-bred members of the species have recently inter-bred with
some of their cousins.*

the door was always locked

except to a few

late night visitors

a slow moving line

of buffed shells

jostling in the moonlight

a sign nailed

to the door post read:

'Knock twice and ask for

Chelonoidis elephantopus'.

112

Small Americans

ten small Americans sitting in a school

one tries to hug a friend

but it's against the rules

nine small Americans standing in a row

two decide to have a chat

but teacher's saying no

seven small Americans playing in the sun

three would like to have a race

but they're not allowed to run

four small Americans with lots of life to give

but they've forgotten that they're children

and lost the will to live

no small Americans...

Speeding offence

there once was a couple who, in two thousand and
three

shared practically everything, they were married you
see

it was seen as supporting each other, they thought

their principles stood up; they were rigid and taut

then some motorway madness put it all to the test

when one broke the speed limit, but the other
confessed

now divorcees, they're sitting back to back in the dock

one wears the trousers, the other a frock

no-one pleads guilty and they're bailed to appear

on Crimewatch, The News and next season's Top
Gear

Spun

A four metre piece of fabric and a cape, created from silk spun by over one million Golden Orb spiders went on show at London's Victoria and Albert Museum. It took more than five years to weave.

"Brothers and sisters of S.P.I.N. *(Silk Producers In Need)*

we are all victims of a ruthless capitalist world!

It is said our webs are a miracle of the natural world and yet,

even though we work tirelessly all our lives

to construct them, they are torn down and

woven into ornaments for the rich and powerful.

And all this without the statutory tea breaks,

holidays and worst of all, no final salary pension scheme.

Well I say to you fellow arachnids, enough is enough;

it's time for action; to get proper rights for spiders everywhere.

It's time to strike; to protect our species

from permanent slavery.

Are you with me brothers and sisters,

are you with me...alright, all those in favour?

NO... not all eight!!!"

Stormbirds

(beachcombing 6)

they took off

flew the twisting sand

suddenly

long before

anything else and

circled, crying

from the clouds

vanishing

when the wind

eventually blew

the wave tops,

clattering creels

against men and

scrubbing skin

blood clean

as the storm faded

feathers

tickled the dawn

in a calm

drying drift

Sweetener

one granule of sugar is

instantaneous on the tongue

which then craves more

suck a finger

dip it into the sugar bowl

and suck again

kiss your fist before

punching the sweetness

from other tongues

promise more sugar

promise more promise

but never lick your lips

Tall Flame

(Nelson Mandela – 2012)

a tall flame

still burning over peace

flickers, blown

on a tall wind

smoke swirling

over an erosion

of rocks.

Its light fading

that dimming blade

still cuts a

deep truth

still stirs the

hearts of a nation

to beat stronger.

Tears Will Never Dry

Two men were finally convicted of the murder of Stephen Lawrence; eighteen years after the attack on the teenager in south east London.

eighteen in Eltham

eighteen in Jamaica

nineteen ninety three, in Jamaica

two thousand and twelve

in Eltham

the world spins

some justice at last

but time turns its back

and scowls

a mother grants no

forgiveness

a father will not

rest, until time

returns and dries

their tears

The Bar

Gripping the well worn handle, I pushed open the door and walked into the bar.

"Dad?"

"Yes, Josh."

"Dad, what did the man say when he walked into the bar?"

"Don't know."

"Ouch!"

The memory vanished as soon as the bar I was walking into, struck me. It was the smell of stale alcohol, together with the sound of 'The Chain' by Fleetwood Mac that greeted me at first. Then as my eyes adjusted to the muted lighting, I could make out a small curved counter on the back wall. I made my way across to it and ordered a double scotch from the barman; gulping half of it before taking a proper look around me. The bar was empty, apart from me, and in need of a lick of paint. No, it was more than that, it needed a complete makeover. A couple of dowdy pictures prowled forlornly across the faded wallpaper, alongside a few sparsely dressed shelves. The dark furniture had, at some time been polished to oblivion, but was now gripped by an ageing greasy dust that sucked the light from the room. The grubby upholstery clung bravely to life against all the odds. I turned to rest my elbows on the sticky bar surface; it was then that I noticed the mirror. It was huge;

covering the entire wall behind the bar and upon it, someone at sometime had very cleverly attached the optics and built small shelves across its surface. When originally installed, it had probably been quite impressive, but now it was just depressing; a miserable reflection of its surroundings.

Although the size and position of the mirror had initially grabbed my attention, it was the reflection that now held my interest and the more I stared at it, the deeper my mood became. I tried, but could not tear my gaze away from the man seated at the bar. I drained my glass and he did the same, mockingly. That wasn't going to help. Wasn't it drinking that had started all the trouble in the first place? The man in the mirror ordered another drink which arrived with commendable speed.

"Crap pub, good service." The man in the mirror said, cradling the drink safely in his hands.

"Bastard!" I hissed at him; as the glass was raised and lowered. "Why did you do it, you stupid thick bastard...why?" He raised a finger to inspect a small cut just over his right eye and to the bruising that was beginning to colour the skin around it.

"It's no more than you deserve," I said. "In fact, Carol let you off pretty lightly if you ask me. You shouldn't even be here."

The man in the mirror glanced around the bar. "Wherever here is!"

I could not answer the question. I wasn't even sure what type of question it was. My mind had, some time now, begun to digest its own ability to reason; to think clearly, with the exception of one thing.

"Another drink, Sir?" The barman.

"Yes, thanks." Another scotch appeared, then after a short while another. The alcohol was beginning to bite now; I recognised the signs. The reflection in the mirror distorted into a hideous reflection of a nightmare I'd been having recently. I'm cringing beneath an upturned whisky tumbler fighting for breath, while a crowd of women and children beat on the glass, trying to get at me; their fists bloody and broken.

Was I losing my mind, or had I lost it already? All through this, the man in the mirror sat opposite me, calm and unaffected by the maelstrom around him. I began to loathe this man more and more. I wanted him to go away forever; to leave me and my life alone.

"Give me another scotch," I slurred "Make it a large one this time."

The barman gave me a look which said, 'I think you've had enough', but he served the drink anyway. The figure in the mirror downed it with one flick of his hand, banging the glass down.

"Again!" I demanded." Sorry Sir..." began the barman.

"Just do it," I repeated, "I've got the money."

"It's not that Sir, it's just ..." he looked nervously at my dark expression. I wasn't bothered though; I was staring at the mirror again. Carol and Josh were standing next to the man now, with their arms around him as if posing for a family portrait; except that they didn't smile. Josh spoke: "What did the man say when he walked into a bar, dad?"

"I...I...don't know."

"C'mon dad what did he say?" They stared at me together, waiting for the answer; but I just couldn't remember. The man they called dad knew though. But he just sat there grinning. Why didn't he tell me the answer?

"What do I say; what can I say?" I shouted at them. I couldn't remember. "I'm so sorry; I'm so, so sorry!"

The man in the mirror was then saying sorry as well; over and over again: "Sorry, sorry, sorry, sorry..."

I was beginning to get scared now. Carol and Josh began to echo the chant. But the tone they used said, 'We're sorry for you; for what you are; for the suffering to come'. I couldn't bare it any longer. I needed another drink. I slammed the glass onto the bar once more.

"Just give me another bloody double." But even as I shouted the words, I knew it was too late. I raised my hand, still clutching the tumbler and flung it at the grinning monster opposite me. It smashed against the

125

mirror leaving a crazy weave of cracks on its surface. A few flakes of silver fluttered onto the shelf below.

For a second or two there was silence. I couldn't see, even though my eyes were open. The world was black. Then a voice filtered through as the darkness faded and I could see the barman at the telephone on the counter.

"...yes, Police please."

Almost immediately the door from the street opened and two police officers walked into the bar (ouch). The barman's mouth dropped open in surprise as I started to laugh. I stopped as one of the officer's spoke:

"Stephen Boyle?"

I nodded; it was me.

"Well, Sir, we'd like to ask you some questions, would you come with us please."

I stood up and walked, rather unsteadily to the door with them. As I reached it, I paused and turned to look back. The barman was picking up pieces of glass from the shelf under the mirror and putting them onto a sheet of newspaper. As I watched, he cursed, raised one of his fingers to his mouth and sucked it. I felt a guiding hand on my elbow; it was time to go and I walked out of the bar and into the darkness.

End

The Crying Bones of Onagawa

ghosts search for their echoes

across a flat wash of land

nothing halts the cry

tiny fragments of lives

driven to the mountains

by unchallenged winds

vertical surfaces like

un-spat broken teeth

shovel familiar shadows

into holes

where they wait for

the finding of memory

The Gates of Sobibor

a tall staircase

trod by many

quickly, but slowly enough

to remember

a set of gates

crying open

on their hinges

twenty eight thousand

stout memories

fifty six thousand

brittle arms

reaching out

welcome

Herr Demjanjuk

The Hungry Baker

my mother sends me a message

to drink milk or

to eat just a little

she is my mother

my throat is closing but

my voice grows stronger as

the food she brings

goes stale beside the bed

my body gets weaker but

my jailors grow weaker still

as they chew and swallow

each mouthful of my Jihad

my cause is proven,

my final loaf baked

The Last Drop

a humble tumbler waits

for the last drop

of a fortunate life

it's not the cupboard's fault

the door opens easily enough

a little squeak maybe, as it closes,

to celebrate the occasion

perhaps an echo from within

a banging of years; a ring

of sticky truth from better times

it's not the bottle's fault either

the cork eases from the neck

pops between the fingers,

sighs from the floor

a seal of approval maybe

a nod from the past

but no better than the last

and the last and

the last

Theft

A sixteen year old girl committed suicide

as a protest at her forced marriage, to the man who raped her.

so this man decided

he would open my legs

like a shop door

and steal everything

he pushed his way into me

pushed his way into my life

now others

are pushing him in again

into my life

into me

my life is now his

he can have it

I don't want it anymore

Through the Walls

Two years after a massive earthquake, which devastated the Caribbean country of Haiti; it was reported that more than five hundred thousand people were still living in makeshift tented villages.

I can see

the Presidential palace and

the Cathédrale de Port-au-Prince

from here

through the walls

of my home

I can see

the Hotel Oloffson

and the foreign reporters

arriving and departing

I can see

members of the government

passing by in their cars

on their way to important meetings

I can see

the walls of other houses

rising from the dust

but mine

remains as dust

Thusha Kamaleswaran - Ballerina

I am a little white cloud

laughing with the sun

playing hide and seek

with the moon

a butterfly

fluttering amongst

embroidered flowers

humming with bees

I am an autumn leaf

warming a forest floor

passing golden light

through my body

a snowflake

drifting over

a million pointes

of taffeta frost

dans mes rêves

32 fouettés en tournant

Tony Nicklinson

(January 23rd 2012)

my hand will not hold a sword

or shoulder bear a rifle's butt

I cannot carry out an order

march off to war and

stand before my enemies

speak of peace or

salute an abeyance of hostilities, so

in death

I will fight on

Township

corrugated sun

the house wall

burns her back

as she watches

the children playing

on the banks

of the town ditch

picking paper flowers

from the mud

chasing plastic butterflies

in the dust

day's work finished

on aching bones

wind flap skirts

under old knits

gathered on the reluctant grass

thinking through

a century

watching over

understanding

enjoying the thin edge

of freedom

Trigger

Violent demonstrations broke out

in Afghanistan, after American troops

burnt copies of the Koran at Bagram air base.

some God book it is

where the words

can be drawn and

fired from a gun

the bullets

suited to their target

fused and detonated

by a twist of doctrine

or a shuffle of values

some faith it is

where love sleeps

one finger on the trigger

where switchback passion

suits every occasion and

can load and prime

its children with hatred

not by education

but by subjugation

Twenty First Century Man

from crawling

to walking

putting one foot

in front of another

we move forward

gathering speed

one day we may run

tripping ourselves up

thinking

which foot first

burning our knees

as we pray

Twenty Year Prayer

On March 14th 1992 eleven men were killed

in an accident while being transported by helicopter,

from the Cormorant Alpha platform.

prayer

a twenty year

reach into the past

pause

a way for spirits

to touch hearts

seed

a scattering of love

into souls

find

a way back

for memories

Two Deaths

A twenty year old is charged with the

murder of a young student,

by shooting him in the head at point black range.

one bullet, two deaths

two deaths and

two mother's grief

in their wasted years

twenty and twenty three years

two lives ended

before beginning

Kiaran and Anuj

babies again

Up Town Girls

Stella and I flopped down onto the carriage seats and with strained smiles, jointly exhaled sighs of relief. That had been a nightmare!

The jazzy upholstery was grubby and covered with stains and I wondered what some of the stains could be, but right now these were definitely the best seats on the train! You know what it's like, when you get onto a train at the end of a long day and it's the train that's going to take you home; that barring any major misfortune, the day is effectively over and all you have to do is sit back and enjoy the journey. It's a lovely feeling and suddenly we felt all the strain and trauma of our ordeal, begin to dissipate.

-o-

After an exciting day out; shopping in the west end of London, we headed down into the underground to start our journey to Kings Cross station. I'd always found the tube a little bit intimidating, no matter what time of day it was. If it was the rush hour, then I would get an overwhelming feeling of claustrophobia; if it was quiet then paranoia would set in and I would regard every fellow passenger as a potential mugger or rapist. I was glad of Stella's company.

As we traipsed down the tunnel into the clammy atmosphere, alongside a few early commuters, I could feel my throat drying and my tongue sticking to the roof of my mouth. It was illogical; I tried to tell myself, to be so nervous. Thousands of people travelled by tube every day and nothing ever happened to them. Ahead of us I could see an old woman sitting with her back against the grey tiled wall, surrounded by a mound of assorted carrier bags. She was dressed in a filthy green parka coat, its hood pulled tightly around her ruddy, weathered face. She was picking at her blackened teeth with grimy fingernails; examining whatever it was she had chiselled out, before flicking it into the air. As Stella and I drew closer, she seemed to loose interest in her oral hygiene and looking up slowly, fixed me with a bloodshot stare. Her eyes followed me as we approached and when we drew level, she threw back her head, opened her awful mouth and let out a single, very loud, *"Ha!"*

Despite the clatter of footsteps and rush of air from the tracks below, the tunnel reverberated to the sound of her voice. The other travellers gave the old woman a nervous look and hurrying passed, pretended to be deep in conversation; either with the person next to them or the person on the mobile phone that they had clamped to one of their ears. I was not so lucky.

"fukkintart, binshoppin avye? fukkinbitch!"

The verbal assault took me by surprise, even though I'd always expected something like this would happen. My heart began to pound in my chest as I looked at

Stella; my eyes pleading for her help. She looked at me, mouth wide open in dismay. She shrugged her shoulders, what could she do? We simultaneously tightened our fingers around the handles of our bags and quickened our pace.

"youandyergirlfrenlezziesareyer?" she shouted; her words flapped like a dirty, ripped flag.

"offorashag, backatyerdesignerflat, eh?"

As we passed, she got to her feet and with surprising agility grabbed her bags. Then to our complete horror, she fell into a rather unsteady lope along side us. She leaned in close as we again upped our pace and straining her filthy face up towards mine, she shouted again; the appalling smell of bad teeth, cider and stale tobacco making my head swim.

"fancyafreesomdarlin, eh? yerjustmytype!"

Panic set in and jerking my head away from the stench, I turned and whisper-screamed into Stella's ear, "For Christ sake, run!"

We picked up our feet and fled down the slope towards the platforms. The others around us looked on; their expressions a mixture of fear and at the same time relief, because the old hag had picked on us and not them. At the bottom of the tunnel we slithered to an undignified halt; confronted by a t-junction. To the right and left were the entrances onto the different platforms. Stella and I looked at the confusing array of signs and then at each other; our eyes wide with uncertainty.

"Which one?" I shouted. "Which one?"

"Aaahhh, this one...I think." Stella faltered and we dived through the left hand gate and onto the packed platform.

We found a small space to stand in; between two city types and dumped our bags onto the concrete floor.

"Did you see what happened to her?" I said, struggling for breath and straining my neck around in all directions.

"No, I can't see her; she must have given up the chase"

"What a horrible old cow. Did you see the state of her, and what about her breath?"

Stella smiled, exhaling deeply, "I was lucky; I didn't get that close; but she really liked you!"

I smiled back, still looking nervously up and down the platform. "She's probably picking on some other poor bastard, thank God!"

Just then, with a rush of air and a screech of brakes a train pulled into the station. Even before it had stopped, we joined the scrum of elbows and armpits, as everyone shuffled towards the doors, all fighting to get on. Stella and I had just squeezed ourselves inside when with a whoosh, the doors closed behind us and we were off into the dark tunnel in a blast of warm, metallic air.

The trip on the tube to King's Cross station was hot, smelly and uncomfortable. All the other passengers looked resigned to the conditions; obviously seasoned tube travellers; whereas Stella and I viewed everyone with suspicion. Even the other females in the carriage seemed threatening; our nerves were so shaky after our earlier encounter. We were so grateful when we finally made it onto the train to Bedford and settled down for the journey home.

-o-

As the train clattered along I was just happy staring out of the window at the familiar scene of unkempt rubbish strewn hedgerows and untidy back gardens. It struck me as odd how some householders could allow their property to get into such a state; especially when it was likely to be gazed at on a regular basis by bored travellers. Stella was thumbing her way through some of the catalogues and magazines that she'd picked up during the day. Somewhere behind us, down the carriage, a connecting door opened and then slammed shut, as a passenger moved towards us along the train. The sound of shuffling feet grew louder as the person, obviously weighed down with shopping, looked for a vacant seat. Probably an elderly person I thought, as I folded up my coat and placed it on the seat next to me, to make it look as if it was taken.

All of a sudden the hairs on the back of my neck stood up and screamed; as a voice I recognised crashed through the peace and quiet of our journey.

"so thereyar, yerunsoshablecows, foughtyercudartrunme didya? well, yerwerong! Visseattakenisit, eh?"

End

VA 92L

an escape

four under the dark

dark sky and

a mother carrying

her babies

through the broken

waters of war

swollen belly but

still trim in the water

seventy years on

still delivering safely

until a reunion

a journey returned

and a restful berth

dry at last

Waiting for the Boats

(beachcombing 7)

we knew tables by colours

by patterns we could name like

Honeysuckle, Willow, Thistle

Pagoda, Morning glory and Diane

incomplete in their beauty but

completely perfect

unmatched, but matchless

the beat of the kitchen's heart

on the harbour wall

we knew boats by colour

our eyes and mouths staring

out to sea

searching for masts

hard stomachs waiting

for fish to land

for those empty plates

to sing

War Correspondent

risk is counted

as a dangerous friend

always approached

with an open hand

and with an exit planned

it is known; it is hard loved

honesty is everything

when you pull the truth

body by body

from the lies;

keeping the camera

focused on the story

send it home quickly; leave

through shattered teeth doors

and torn muslin lives

before you become

the headline;

the story home

Watching Demolition

In Abbottabad north-western Pakistan,

bulldozers began to demolish the house

and the compound where Osama Bin Laden

had been hiding before being shot dead in May 2011.

building a mosque in my heart

I watch the brick and plaster fall

each crumbling wall a failed policy

a release of power

gathered to my breast

while the world breathes dust

my faith is strengthened

as I spit diamonds into the street

and around me, shadows crouch

knees bridged with Kalashnikov's

killing time

killing time

Whitney

danced with us on dusted floors

embraced with us against the stars

curling her voice around our hearts

giving us the strength to dream

she turned us into lovers

with her melodic kiss

healed us with our own memories

scattering touches over broken words

starting fires in cold hearths

Whitney

always our tune on the radio

our partner on life's dance floor

falling in love together

staying in love forever

Zina

she is nearly naked

the dress is torn

ripped apart by years of conflict

centuries of tradition

frayed and split

threads tangle

with each other

wrap around tongues

trip uncertain feet

hypnotise thought

a man waits

needle and cotton

in his hands

but they remain unused

it is woman's work

Other titles by Bernard Briggs

Love, Cry and Wonder Why

A Hatching of Ghosts

Lightning Source UK Ltd.
Milton Keynes UK
UKOW050330290313

208331UK00006B/194/P